The Best Pet

Written by Andrea Shavick

Illustrated by Brett Hudson

At school on Monday, everyone was talking about their pets.

"You should see my cat climb," said Mia.

"My dog's the best at football," said Ali.

"I bet he's not as cute as my hamster," said Emma.

"Or as scary as my snake," said Jamie.

Everyone looked at me.

"Alex hasn't got a pet," said Emma.

"I have!" I shouted. "I have got a pet, and it's better than all of yours!"

"I know," said Ali. "Let's have a competition.
We'll look at the pets after school."

"I'll make a list," said Jamie.

He put me down for Friday.

I didn't say anything.

I haven't really got a pet.

After school we all went to Emma's house. Her hamster was cute, but it didn't want to play or anything. It just wanted to sleep! Emma was cross when I laughed.

"We'll see if *your* pet is any better," she said.

That night I asked Mum,
"Please can I have a pet? Please?"
But Mum said no. Mum always says no.
What was I going to do?

After school on Tuesday, everyone went
home with Ali.

We played football with his dog,
but the man next door got very cross.

"Stop that dog barking!" he shouted.

We had to stop playing and go home.

After school on Wednesday, everyone went
home with Mia to see her cat Tinkerbell.

"Climb that tree Tinkerbell, climb!"
we shouted. Tinkerbell climbed.

"Oh no!" said Mia. "She's stuck!"

"Not again," sighed Mia's dad.
"I'd better ring the fire brigade."

That night I went next door to Mr Silver's.

"Please may I borrow your parrot
on Friday?" I said.

"Aargh, I'm sorry," said Mr Silver.
"He's got talking lessons on Friday."

What was I going to do?

After school on Thursday, we all went to Jamie's house to see his snake.

HISS! HISS!

His snake was so scary we ran away!

Emma looked at me.

"Is your pet scary?" she laughed.

I wasn't worried. I had a plan.

That night I did some hunting around the back garden.

Now I had a pet...

...but on Friday morning, it was gone!

"I put your snail back in the garden," said Mum. "It didn't want to live by itself in a box."

After school everyone came home with me. "Where's your pet?" they said.

How could I tell them I didn't have a pet? Suddenly, we heard banging. I had an idea.

"Come on!" I shouted. "This way for the best pet!"

I pushed the door open...

13

...and there was my little brother jumping
up and down in his cot!

"These bars are strong," giggled Emma.
"Is your pet dangerous?"

"Can we play with him?" asked Mia.

"Only if you're very careful," said Mum.

We took my pet for
walks round the garden,
and then we fed him.

My pet made so much mess,
we had to give him a bath. My pet
loves water, so we all got very wet!

Splash
Splash

"That's enough!" said Mum. "I think it's time to put your pet to bed."

"Wait!" shouted Emma. "What about the competition? We haven't judged it yet!"

Can you guess who won?